THE MINDSET OF A RICH MAN:

Discover the secrets to a Rich Man's Success in Life.

Jerome B. Port

All rights reserved. No part of this publication may be reproduced, distributed, or transmitted in any form or by any means, including photocopying, recording, or other electronic or mechanical methods, without the prior written permission of the publisher, except in the case of brief quotations embodied in critical reviews and certain other noncommercial uses permitted by copyright law.

Copyright © Jerome B. Port, 2022.

Table of Contents

Chapter 1

Chapter 2

Chapter 3

Chapter 4

Chapter 5

Chapter 1

The Rich Man Understands and Control His Subconscious Mind

The subconscious is the portion of our thoughts that makes choices without our having to consciously think about them. It's distinct from the conscious mind, which comprises the ideas we know we are thinking at any particular time. It's also distinct from the unconscious mind, which contains prior events and experiences that we don't recall at all.

Learning to play an instrument is a fantastic illustration of how the subconscious mind functions. At first, you need to think about interpreting the sheet music and moving your fingers to play each note, but as you practice, you realize you can pick up any song and play it.

The subconscious mind extends beyond acquiring new abilities. It's engaged in information processing and influences everything we think, say and do. It stores our ideas and values, decides our memories, and monitors the information all around us, determining what to convey to the conscious mind and what to keep for later. It influences every minute of our life — yet most of us don't even realize it.

So how long does it take to rewire your subconscious mind? On average it takes roughly three to four weeks — but it might take longer. The answer will depend on how deeply established the habit is that you wish to modify, as well as your own limiting beliefs.

SHIFTING YOUR MINDSET
To understand how to reprogram your mind for success, there are three actions you must follow that will transform your perspective and guide your concentration in the proper way.

STEP 1: DECIDE

The first step you need to do is to achieve total clarity on what it is you desire. Learn how to avoid overthinking and concentrate on your objectives. What is your intended outcome? What does unleashing an amazing life look like to you? Clarity is power. The more thought you put into this, the more detail you lay down, and the better and more powerful your vision will become. This generates a subconscious mind map, providing your brain with the skills required to transform that vision into reality.

Want to retrain your mind? Consider a dispute with your lover. When in a heated discussion with a loved one, we frequently lose sight of the dispute itself and concentrate on being heard — on gaining the final word, on winning. You stop regulating your tone and being compassionate with your spouse and begin treating them like an opponent.

That's a fast way to escalate the disagreement into something far worse.
Instead, pause yourself and question, "Why am I fighting in the first place?" You aren't fighting to fight; you are disputing about something and want a resolution. When you are sidetracked by winning, you lose focus on the underlying issue. Once you recall that, you may change your attention back to fixing the original issue, essentially rewiring your brain to utilize its resources and accomplish that result in that instant.

Subconscious reprogramming begins with determining what you want – now and in the future – and concentrating on it. Give your intellect direction. Where attention goes, energy flows. What do you desire physically, financially, emotionally, and spiritually in your company and in your personal life? Make the choice that you are not willing to settle and that you are not willing to live the way you are living right now. Set your focus on what you desire and begin rewiring your brain.

subconscious mind

STEP 2: COMMIT
After you select what you want, the next phase of subconscious reprogramming is committing. Rid your thoughts of dread and self-doubt. How do you do that? By committing to it and letting it drive you.

Fear is one of the major traps that inhibit individuals from taking action. We all have fears — fear of rejection, fear of failure, success, suffering, or the unknown. If you do nothing, that fear will stay right where it is, obstructing your progress. You will not move, and you will constantly live in terror. You may not do any worse, but you also won't do better. And that dread will always be there in the back of your mind, driving you away from your ambitions. The absence of action allows the negative time to poison your thoughts: "It's a good thing I didn't attempt. I would never have succeeded. This fear-based negativity will permeate everything you believe about yourself and all you do if allowed to spread via your subconscious mind.

The only way to cope with fear and reprogram your thinking is to meet it head-on. You must stare it in the eye and take action in spite of it. Are you terrified of failure? Look at it this way: Failure is an education. If you do something and fail, you will know what doesn't work. You'll be able to adopt a more educated, informed approach next time. You're better off than where you were previously.

Reprogramming your brain entails breaking through negative chatter such as, "I can't." Think about it the same way you would grow muscle at the gym. At first, it will appear challenging and maybe even exhausting. But if you start modestly and do it every day, you will progressively get stronger. And soon, it will become an easy habit.

Commit to yourself. Commit to overcoming the negative. Commit to a better life. When you commit entirely, closing out every other alternative, you will push yourself to the next level and demand more of yourself than anybody else could possibly anticipate. And it is the actual power of subconscious mind programming.

STEP 3: RESOLVE

Once you have settled on your route and committed wholeheartedly, take inventory of your position. What are your present activities getting you? Direct your thoughts toward examining what is working and what isn't. Make the shifts. Resolve is about finding answers to whatever may come your way.

A vital aspect of establishing resolve and efficiently rewiring your brain is flexibility. Tunnel vision sets constraints on you - you will lose out on chances and other pathways that may lead to amazing rewards. Remember, you are never 100% in control. Consider this: has your life gone exactly as planned? Probably not. The road you travel is seldom a straight line. And that's why it's crucial to stay adaptable along the road — learning from errors, accepting failure, and utilizing negativity as a driving force for development. As long as you are making progress, you are headed in the correct way.

When you retrain your mind to concentrate on determination, you gain the capacity to adapt your approach to challenges as necessary. Not all barriers, hurdles, or conditions are the same; each brings its unique problems, and you may tackle those issues head-on. True strength comes from inside, and rewiring your brain trains you for success. Frustration becomes a blessing since it implies you are on the cusp of a breakthrough. Failure becomes a lesson, coaching you on how to be better in the future. Any hurdle becomes a chance for you to pivot and discover a fresh innovative solution. That is the force of your mind's determination to resolve.

SIX TIPS ON HOW TO REPROGRAM YOUR SUBCONSCIOUS

Now that you're in a strong, determined mood, it's important to develop good behaviors that will reprogram your mind to have entire confidence in itself.

1. ADOPT EMPOWERING BELIEFS

Limiting ideas hold us back from what we desire in life. They might be based on previous outcomes, unfavorable occurrences you've encountered, or a mistaken view of your future. When you confront these beliefs and dispute their veracity, you may replace them with powerful beliefs to live by. What does this look like? It may be switching "My parents were divorced, thus it's in my genetic code to not have a great relationship," to "I deserve a healthy relationship with someone I love." When you alter your self-talk, you change your world.

2. EMBRACE THE BEAUTY OF UNCERTAINTY

We are not in control of life — the only thing we can control is our actions and emotions. When we adopt this thought, we take back our authority to mold our reality and reprogram our thinking. Let go of the demand for certainty and accept the beauty of ambiguity. When we concentrate on choosing trust, giving without worrying about what we're receiving in return, and living mindfully, we can let go and enjoy the trip.

3. FOCUS ON GRATITUDE

When you choose thankfulness and appreciation over criticism and fear, you cast a light on the good. Your brain gets rewired as a result to focus more on what you have rather than what you lack. It also permits you to be intrigued about the happenings in your life since you no longer regard them with skepticism. You may accept change and allow it in, knowing that life never remains the same.

4. WATCH YOUR ENVIRONMENT

When retraining your brain for success, you have to minimize negative influences in your surroundings. Your subconscious mind is continuously gathering information from outside sources and utilizing that knowledge to build ideas that impact how you think and behave. Negativity from the daily news, toxic individuals, and social media may have a huge influence on your subconscious mind without you even knowing it.

As you concentrate on how to reprogram your mind, remember that proximity is power. Surround yourself with positive, supporting individuals. Seek out books, films, and music that raises you up and empowers you. Over time, you will realize that your subconscious mind is more cheerful and encouraging and that negative ideas have substantially lessened.

5. VISUALIZE

Remember the basketball players? They learned how to alter their thoughts via visualization. By envisioning in their thoughts the ideal free throw over and over, they were able to train their brains to really hit such shots once they arrived on the court.

What does your ideal day look like? How do you want your major presentation at work to go? How precisely do you want a first date to go? Pick something you are sincerely devoted to making a reality and spend 10-15 minutes each day picturing it as if it has already occurred. Your subconscious mind will absorb the sentiments in your pictures as if they were genuine, giving you the inner confidence you need to make them come true.

6. BINAURAL BEATS CAN BE USED TO BIOHACK YOUR SUBCONSCIOUS MIND.

Biohacking is combining experiments and technology to enhance your health and well-being. Biohacking might entail red light treatment to boost health, following an intermittent fasting schedule to stimulate weight reduction, or adding supplements to your diet to supercharge your health. One great technique to rewire your mind via biohacking is by leveraging the power of music. Our brainwaves react differently to various forms of music and we may generate particular sensations with the correct rhythms.

Binaural beats entail playing two tones at various frequencies to generate particular states of consciousness. It's been proved that our subconscious mind receives information better when we are in a calm condition, thus you may employ binaural beats to generate alpha brainwaves.

HOW TO KNOW IF IT'S WORKING

Subconscious mind programming may be tough - by its very definition, you can't always know what it's thinking. But there are techniques to know whether your attempts to rewire your mind are succeeding.

You're getting more self-aware. You must be aware of your subconscious mind in order to reprogram it. Are you growing better at preventing negative self-talk and managing your emotions? Are you able to adjust your concentration at will? These are symptoms of self-awareness.

You take greater chances. Everyone has various risk thresholds, yet limiting beliefs drive us not to take any chances at all. When you reprogram your thinking, you'll enhance your confidence and be ready to step out of your comfort zone.

You attract optimism. As Tony says, "Whatever you continually think about and concentrate upon you go toward." That's the law of attraction: retraining your mind to think more favorably will really bring more good things into your life

Chapter 2

The Attitude of the Rich Man

Millionaires have more in common with each other than simply their bank accounts—for some millionaires, hitting it rich takes guts, salesmanship, vision, and passion. Find out which attributes are most frequent among the seven-figure bank account set and what you can do to cultivate some of these talents yourself.

Independent Thinking

Millionaires think differently. Not only about money, but about everything. The time and energy everyone else spends seeking to comply, millionaires spend crafting their own path.

Since thoughts affect actions, those who desire to be affluent should think in a manner that will bring them to that objective. Independent thinking doesn't imply doing the opposite of what the rest of the world is doing; it means having the confidence to pursue what is essential to you. So, the lesson here is to make your own route. Let your success lead you to financial riches rather than doing it the other way around and attempting to chase the money.

For example, David Geffen is a self-made tycoon with $9.9 billion to his name in 2021, according to Forbes. This American record executive and film producer was a college dropout, yet Geffen gained millions by launching record agencies, including DreamWorks Animation SKG Inc., and signed some of the most important bands of the '70s and '80s. Although he didn't pursue what many perceive to be the conventional road to success, his persistent work ethic and sense of personal conviction in artists' potential enabled him to pile up a significant fortune.

Vision

Millionaires are creative visionaries with a good outlook. In other words, affluent individuals have huge goals, and they think they will come true. As such, wealth seekers should set big objectives and not be scared of unexplored ground.

Bill Gates, the world's second-richest person in 2021 with a net worth of $124 billion, according to Forbes, did precisely that. The co-founder of Microsoft delivered personal computers to the public. Gates moved into the personal computers market in 1975 and hung on fast, establishing Microsoft Windows in 1985. When customers started to bring computers into their homes, Gates was poised to benefit from this new technology.

Gates left his position on the Microsoft board in the middle of March 2020. He co-chairs the Bill & Melinda Gates Organization, the world's biggest private charity foundation to which the pair has contributed $35.8 billion worth of Microsoft shares. Gates is also now a fervent speaker and academic on the topic of climate change.

Skills
Writers Dennis Kimbro and Napoleon Hill examined successful individuals to find the attributes they have in common for their book, Think and Grow Rich: A Black Choice (1992). (1992). The authors observed that successful individuals concentrate on their areas of expertise. Millionaires also like to collaborate with others to enhance their lesser talents. If you don't know what you are excellent at, poll friends and relatives. Use training and mentors to enhance your strong talents.

Passion
Billionaire investment genius Warren Buffett says, "Money is a by-product of something I enjoy doing very much." Enjoying your job permits you to have the discipline to work hard at it every day.

People that work with money for a career, bankers, for example, generally adore negotiating new arrangements and convincing others to finish a transaction.

But finding your desired profession may take time, and becoming a billionaire takes time. According to Entrepreneur, even the richest billionaires took an average of eight years to achieve their first million. Not only that, but many endure major failures along the route. Pavle Marinkovic, writing at Medium.com, reveals that Warren Buffett, Steve Ballmer, former Microsoft CEO, and Rupert Murdoch of the Fox media empire, all made big blunders before they became successful.

So, if you want to be wealthy, quit doing things you don't like, and do what you love. If you aren't sure what you adore, try a few things and keep trying until you strike on the correct item.

Investment

Millionaires are prepared to sacrifice time and money to attain their objectives. They are prepared to take a risk today for the chance of reaching something bigger in the future. Investing may involve stocks or launching a business—either way, it is a step toward obtaining huge financial gains. Start investing today.

Salesmanship

Millionaires are continually promoting their ideas and encouraging others to purchase them. A good salesman is indifferent to criticism and skeptics. In other words, they don't accept no for an answer. Millionaires also have strong social skills. In fact, when writer T. Harv Eker reviewed the findings of a poll of 753 millionaires for his book, Secrets of the Millionaire Mind (2005), he discovered social skills were more crucial than IQ.

The capacity to interact with others is vital to marketing your concept. Contrary to the usual notion of salespeople, millionaires mention honesty as a significant aspect of their success. If you want to be a billionaire, be an honest salesperson, and perfect your social skills.

Becoming a millionaire is not a goal that can be reached immediately for most individuals. In truth, many of the world's wealthiest individuals amassed their money over many years (sometimes even decades) by making sensible but frequently risky choices, putting their abilities to the greatest use possible, and tirelessly following their goals. If you can learn anything from millionaires, it's that for many of them, their wealth is not necessarily what sets them apart from the rest of the world—what it's they did to get those millions that truly stands out.

Chapter 3

Why does the Rich Man have more than one stream of income?

The demand for multiple income streams has never been greater. Since no employment is secure in the present economic environment, having many sources of income may help us diversify our risks and make sure we're never without money.

More and more people are developing several revenue streams for themselves via side jobs or passive income sources. For good reason, having several cash flow sources is now highly regarded. There are a number of advantages, such as increased financial stability, debt repayment, and more.

Here are some excellent arguments for why it would be smart for you to add more sources of income to your budget.

More stable financial situation

Workplaces undergo fast change. Unexpected layoffs and job loss may happen to people for reasons that are entirely out of their control. Having many sources of income means you have a backup plan. You have a backup plan in case your primary source of money fails. Having many sources of income alleviates some of the financial hardship that job loss might entail.
helps reduce debt

It may be challenging to pay off debt, particularly if you have a variety of debts, such as credit card debt, a mortgage, or a car loan. Paying down these loans each month might be challenging, particularly if the interest rates are high. You may be able to avoid paying a lot of interest by making additional payments on current debt, which can also hasten the repayment process.

Supports Living Within Your Means

You must be able to live within your means if you want to grow your fortune. You need to either spend less money or earn more if you want to live within your means. With inflation and growing prices, it might be particularly difficult to reduce spending. Adding a second source of income may help you cover more costs and increase your savings and investments if you are unable to further reduce your spending.

Increased Inflation

The cost of living has increased as a result of inflation. Gas costs and grocery store prices have been most negatively impacted. Pay and salaries often do not keep pace with inflation. In fact, the majority of Canadians claim that growing prices are taking over their money.

Paying for greater daily expenses may be greatly aided by adding a second source of income. You'll have additional cash on hand to use for necessities and to contribute to your savings and investments.

Possibility of Working Less

Having extra sources of income may allow you to work less. You may have more freedom in how many hours you need to work if you have passive income from investments, digital goods, and online courses.

Maybe you won't have to put in extra hours or wear yourself out to receive a raise. Without having to worry whether you will have enough money to handle this month's bills, you can spend more time doing the things you enjoy and concentrating on more interesting methods to create your own money.

Become financially independent

Financial freedom may come in many different ways. Financial freedom might include paying off debt, having enough money for retirement, and other things. There are many options.

You will provide yourself with alternatives for yourself and your work that you probably wouldn't have otherwise by developing and maintaining various sources of income. Perhaps you could accept a position with more flexible hours, even if it meant forgoing some of your pay. It can imply that you can switch to a part-time job. Future financial worries might be alleviated by having many sources of income.

Chapter 4

A Rich Make Money Works for Him.

Money is a tool that may allow you to attain your objectives. It may bring comfort and security for your family, make it simpler to prepare for the future, and enable you to save towards crucial milestones. But to attain these goals, you need to know how to make your money work for you.

What Does It Mean To Make Your Money Work For You?

Making your money work for you requires taking control of your finances, then utilizing that control to consistently increase your financial stability and security. You may finally be able to obtain financial independence or generate wealth via investment. But none of those things can happen without first knowing where your money is going and finding better methods to utilize it.

Learn To Budget
A budget is a key tool for improving the way you manage your money.
When you are budgeting, you understand where your money is coming from and are strategic about where you spend it. You are making your money do what you want it to do, rather than spending without a strategy.
Note: The purpose of budgeting is to constantly spend less than you earn.
When you build a budget, you allocate every dollar you make to a spending category. You may use a budget to:

Reduce your expenditures
Understand where your money is going
Identify unhealthy financial behaviors
Pay off debt
Avoid generating new debt

Prioritize spending on items that are important to you
Save for the future

Budgeting is not a one-time activity. It should be something you actively participate in every day. You may need to change your budget from month to month to accommodate major costs or your personal spending patterns.

When you know how much revenue you have, you may determine where to put it. When you are intentional about where you spend it, you are in charge of your money. This is the first step towards making it operate the way you want it to, rather than feeling dominated by your money.

Get Out of Debt
When you are in debt, you pay more than the amount of the initial transaction. You also have to make interest payments that might drastically eat into your income.

Debt implies your money isn't working for you, it's going towards paying that interest. It causes a financial burden and restricts the options that you may make.

Paying off debt, by contrast, enables you to take that money and channel it toward the things that are essential to you. You may apply the money toward other financial objectives, such as saving for college, developing a retirement fund, traveling, or changing your living circumstances. You can start a company. You may begin investing it, enabling you to expand your money and achieve greater financial security and freedom.

If you have a lot of debt and are feeling overwhelmed, you may utilize the snowball approach to regulate the debt payback process.
Pay just the minimum payment on all your debts and save the lowest one.

Put any additional money you have toward paying down the lowest debt.

Once it's paid off, proceed to the next smallest.

As you pay off your lesser bills, you'll have more money available to pay off your bigger ones. This momentum helps you concentrate your efforts and get out of debt more rapidly.

Create an Emergency Fund

Surprises are terrifying when you do not have control of your money. An unexpected auto repair, a medical operation, a job loss, or any other financial disaster may rapidly send you tumbling into new or greater debt, wiping away any progress you've made toward regaining control of your money.

Creating an emergency fund is another method to make your money work for you since it shows you have arranged for shocks. If an emergency does come to arise, you may put the money in your fund to work and recover control of the situation.

Building emergency savings might take time. Ideally, you should save aside three to six months' worth of earnings.. But any little you can lay away will help. If you are still paying off debt or don't have much wiggle room in your budget, put aside whatever you can in an "unexpected costs" area in your budget. At the end of the month, transfer whatever is in this category to a separate savings account.

Note

Put your emergency funds in a high-yield savings account, which will generate more interest than a typical savings or checking account. This implies that the money you save will earn money while it's sitting in your bank account. If your bank doesn't offer high-yield accounts or you reside in a remote location without a bank, seek internet banking choices to start an account.

Once you are out of debt or have more free money in your budget, you may set up bigger regular payments to develop your emergency fund even quicker.

Note
Put your emergency funds in a high-yield savings account, which will generate more interest than a typical savings or checking account. This implies that the money you save will earn money while it's sitting in your bank account. If your bank doesn't offer high-yield accounts or you reside in a remote location without a bank, seek internet banking choices to start an account.

In addition to an emergency fund, you will also require retirement funds. You should also consider if you require:
Education funds, for yourself or your children
Travel savings

A down payment fund for a home
Savings to start a business
An automobile fund, for maintenance or a new vehicle
Extracurricular fund for dependents
Long-term care savings, for yourself or dependents
By setting dedicated savings accounts, you may measure your progress toward certain targets. You may also place your funds in a high-interest account, money market account, or CD (certificate of deposit) in order to receive interest on your money.

Note
Remember, anytime you pay interest, you are losing money. But when you earn interest, your money is creating additional money all by itself.

If you won't need your savings for many years or decades, one of the greatest ways to make your money work for you is to invest.

When you put your money into investments, it grows all on its own via interest or the rising worth of the product you invested in. Some investments also generate dividends, which you may either accept as additional money or reinvest to help your portfolio expand.

Note
Investing is a long-term approach to developing wealth. The most successful investors invest early, then let their money develop for years or decades before utilizing it as income. Constantly purchasing and selling stocks is likely to produce less money than a buy-and-hold approach in the long term.

As you start investing, it is crucial to diversify your portfolio. Having all your money in just one sort of investment increases your risk. If that one investment fails, all your money might be gone. Instead, spread that risk out by investing in a variety of:

Stocks Exchange-traded funds (ETFs) (ETFs)
Government bonds
Mutual funds
Real estate Business (your own or someone else's)

Note
Many mutual funds or brokerage companies impose a minimum sum for first-time investors. You may need to save up that minimal amount before you start investing. In the interim, you may start small using investing applications that enable you to acquire fractional shares by investing sums as little as $1 at a time.

No matter how you are saving or investing, have a precise set of objectives. Know what you are working towards, like paying for your child's school, buying a house, or early retirement. This can help concentrate your spending and offer you inspiration, as well as help you select what sorts of investments are the greatest for you.

Chapter 5

How a rich man overcomes obstacles.

Not Having Clear Financial Goals

Have you ever simply driven your automobile without a clear goal in mind? If you ever do this, more often than not, you will wind up driving in circles and end up getting nothing. It is the same with investing. If you do not have clearly defined objectives such as an investment aim or a reason for investing, you are unlikely to achieve financially.

For example, Joe never had clear savings or investing objectives in mind hence he never came up with a solid strategy. Instead, if Joe had established a clear aim like saving $2,000 per month for the next 12 months, he would have been more likely to come up with a feasible strategy to make it happen.

This is why you need to find out things like why you are investing or saving, how much are you going to save, how long are you investing/saving for, etc. before you can come up with a strategy to attain your financial objective. You should also bear in mind that while giving oneself financial objectives you need to be reasonable. If you set yourself unachievable objectives, you will set yourself up for failure and it is a mistake that is best avoided.

Inability to Control Spending

This is by far the most prevalent impediment to becoming financially successful. Spending impulsively is a sure-shot method to demolish whatever financial goals that you may have in place. If you do not think or prepare effectively before you spend, you will constantly miss your financial objectives.

Sadly, there is no expenditure tracker App in the world that can genuinely make you manage your impulse to spend. So, you have to manage yourself. One alternative technique to curb your temptation to spend is to ask yourself to provide an honest response to the question – "Do I truly need it?" and behave appropriately.

Trying to Chase High Returns
It is human nature to compare our performance to that of others and if you discover that your returns are lower than those of your friend's or family member's, you can end up altering your investments. This drive to pursue big returns, might cause you to make frequent changes to your assets and not allow your present investments enough time to thrive. This is particularly true in the case of Equity Mutual Fund investments that are prone to short-term volatility but have the potential to enhance your wealth considerably in the long run.

So instead of attempting to chase large profits, you should remain engaged in the long run and give your assets adequate time to develop. But please bear in mind that you must also make an effort to routinely assess the performance of your present assets and make adjustments only if absolutely required.

Inadequately Planning for Emergencies
Emergencies are a feature of life and insufficiently preparing for them might hinder you from attaining your financial objectives. Two main things you must do to be financially ready for emergencies- obtain enough Health Insurance and create an emergency fund.
If you have appropriate Health Insurance, you will guarantee your bank balance doesn't reach zero in case of a medical emergency. Also, you spare yourself from the potential of bearing large debt on your shoulders in order to pay the payments.

While health crises may be dealt with insurance, there are other emergencies like job loss that could happen. As a result, you should have an emergency fund as well. An emergency fund will help you to sail through challenging times without worrying about money. But please mind that you need to have a large enough amount of money. That's why it is advisable that you keep at least 12 month's costs as your emergency reserve. To guarantee that emergency funds are quickly accessible, try distributing them equally among Liquid Funds or Overnight Funds and your bank account.

www.ingramcontent.com/pod-product-compliance
Lightning Source LLC
Chambersburg PA
CBHW071148240526
45465CB00024BA/2026